ADDRESS.

CLASSICAL LEARNING AS AN ELEMENT OF MODERN SCHOLARSHIP.

AN

ADDRESS

DELIVERED BEFORE THE

EROSOPHIAN SOCIETY,

OF

LOMBARD UNIVERSITY,

ON

TUESDAY, JUNE 18th, 1867,

BY

AUSTIN ADAMS.

PUBLISHED BY REQUEST.

Dubuque:

BARNES & RYAN, PRINTERS, TIMES BOOK AND JOB PRINTING HOUSE.

1867.

ADDRESS.

Ladies and Gentlemen: The occasion which has called us together marks the close of another Academic year of this University. To its friends and patrons here assembled, I take the liberty, in the name of the Erosophian Society, which has selected me as its orator, to extend a greeting. To the members of the society, and to the students of the university in general, I may say in behalf of the friends and visitors, of whom the speaker is one, it affords us pleasure to meet you. Released for a day from the cares of business, we have gathered in this classic retreat,—some to renew old college friendships, and others to manifest their respect for the young men and women whose term of study is now completed. These literary reunions furnished by our college and university commencements, are oases in the barren plains of our dusty, over-wrought, business lives. It is well to return occasionally to refresh our spirits in the scholarly associations of our earlier manhood. Yet the main object of this occasion is not recreation. We should sadly misappropriate it, if some word were not said, and some thought suggested, in the interest of that higher learning which this university was founded to promote.

The magnificent endowment of one hundred thousand dollars recently secured has impressed me with the idea that something should be said upon the completeness of that education that will be commensurate with the foundation upon which this university is about to be placed.

There is a growing tendency among the students of our American colleges and universities to adopt what is called a partial course of study, and that course, it will be found, is mainly scientific. The importance of what is deemed practical is unduly exalted. To this idea all symmetry of education is necessarily sacrificed. The term liberal, as applied to learning, is fast losing its significance. All education, it is thought, must have a sort of special or professional character. It must look towards business. Special aptitudes must be cultivated. Idiosyncracies must be nursed and developed. If a young man or woman lacks mental balance, it is made the business of the schools to see to it that mental balance is placed beyond recovery. So the beauty and harmony of life is sacrificed, and the world is being filled with unbalanced men;—with brilliant pettifoggers, demagogues, quacks and charlatans.

Regretting this tendency to depart from the good old college course of study that rounded out the lives of our fathers into such beauty and symmetry, however moderate their attainments, and believing that the antidote demanded by the over-practical tendency of modern civilization, is to be found in the cultivation of the taste, the sentiments and emotions, and above all in communion with the classic spirit which contrasts so finely with our own, I beg leave to invite your attention to the subject of Classical Learning as an Element of Modern Scholarship.

The oldest colleges in this country were founded by men who were educated in Europe. They consequently became animated, in a great measure, by the same spirit which prevailed in the colleges of Europe. A complete course of study was insisted on. That patience and thoroughness which characterize everything in the old world, were manifested in nothing American so much as in American colleges.

No young man went to college without having first counted upon, and provided for, the cost of a complete course of study. Nothing but sickness or death, or some unforeseen event of controlling importance, cut him short in his course. Of whatever size might be a class when it entered, of that size—with two, three or four deducted for sickness and death—it graduated. The students pursued the same studies and received the same degree. But those old world ideas of thoroughness and completeness were not quite in harmony with that impatience, haste and superficiality of ours, which are distinctively American. Not readily however did the old world spirit in our colleges yield to the American. But colleges in this country became numerous, and were not well endowed or patronized. They sprang up on every side, not so much in obedience to the demands of liberal learning as the offspring of sectarian zeal or of local ambition. Soon they were tempted to lower their standard by providing a partial course. The temptation came in the form of a whole army of short-sighted, impatient students, with cheap, American ideas, demanding that such provision should be made. This demand was backed largely by the newspaper press of the country, and by men who had achieved wealth and influence with a limited education. The first, or among the first, to yield, strange to say, was Brown University, notwithstanding its wealth and age, and its proud and glorious record. Others followed in quick succession, and now, I suppose, more than half of our colleges have provided a partial course. And so well pleased are the American people with this state of things, it is of no use now to discuss its expediency. But while we accept the situation, it becomes the advocates of liberal learning to make greater efforts to save our students from the seductive influence of the times, and to keep them up out of the partial course, towards which they gravitate so strongly. The age is ultilitarian, and in the West this characteristic is intensified. Nor is it difficult to discover the reason. Will a Chicago man, for instance, stop to analyze Greek verbs, or even to recreate himself in the pleasures of the immortal Iliad, when in ten years, if he but seize the golden opportunity, he may acquire a fortune that will build him a house on Michigan Avenue, and give him a controlling interest in the First, Second or Third National Bank? Should we expect an Iowa farmer to linger over the pages of Horace or the Bucolics of Virgil, when wheat is worth two dollars a bushel, and the garden of the world is spread before him waiting to be tilled? We are utilitarian on account of the rapid development of our physical resources, and the opportunity for the sudden acquisition of wealth. And so strong is this drift of the times, it can neither be controlled or checked by anything that can be said by commencement orators, or college Presidents or Professors. Nevertheless, conceding to the age that the main thing in life is to get rich, and that everybody can do it, there is one thing that should not be said without a protest, and that is that liberal culture as the result of early classical study is not valuable. As that has been said, we come here to utter our protest. If men resolve that they will build their marble fronts, though at the cost of somewhat of the completeness of their manhood, it becomes us to consider here, upon this day, which is consecrated not to bank stocks, nor railroads, nor houses, what that cost is.

Before proceeding however to speak of the value of a classical education, we will consider for a moment two causes which have contributed to impair its value in the popular estimation. The first is the developement and achievements of modern science, and the second is the richness of modern literature.

It is not too much to say that to modern science we are indebted principally for the valuable characteristics of modern civilization. Even those things seemingly remote, liberal principles in government and a liberal, progressive theology, have resulted, in a measure, from the amelioration of the physical condition of men, to say nothing of the more direct influence which scientific inquiries have had upon liberal thought. When we rise up and when we lie down, modern science administers to our comfort. It has strengthened human hands and feet and eyes ten thousand fold. By removing our physical limitations, it has given equal freedom to the soul.

It is not my purpose to dwell on the importance or brilliancy of recent scientific discoveries. This subject has afforded the material with which innumerable discourses have been pointed and embellished, and I cheerfully concede all that the devotees of science have claimed. But there is one fact in this connection not sufficiently considered. Scientific discoveries and the study of known science are not the same. Let the boundaries of science be enlarged. Let Nature be compelled to give up her secrets, for in this direction lies the grand march of human progress. But the discoveries once made, it is not equally important that every student should follow them out in all their ramifications. It is, to be sure, important to any person to know the principle upon which the steam engine acts, but the great thing was done when it was substituted for the puny muscles of men and animals in the gigantic pursuits of modern commerce and manufactures. Let me not be misunderstood. I merely say that the value of scientific discoveries and the value of the study of known science as a study, cannot be estimated by any common standard. To estimate the value of a study as a study, entirely different elements enter into the calculation. For this purpose, we consider to what extent it furnishes valuable information; to what extent it disciplines the reason, the memory, the imagination; to what extent it improves the taste, and to what extent it awakens and refines the emotional in man. Nor is this all: we must go still farther, and consider the peculiar kind of discipline it gives the reason, memory and imagination; the peculiar kind of improvement it affords the taste, and the peculiar manner in which it awakens and refines the emotional. Having determined all this, another question of equal importance arises: what place shall a given study occupy in a programme of study, so as to secure the most complete, harmonious, and symmetrical development and genial culture of all the faculties? To determine this, requires a knowledge of mind, the order in which the different faculties are properly developed, and the peculiar effect of each study in the programme. Scientific studies therefore instead of being so important that they should be allowed to crowd out other studies, are simply a part of the disciplinary means by which a liberal education is secured. They are an absolutely necessary part to be sure, but they are counterparts of entirely different studies to be used in the disciplinary process. The question of their rank, therefore, is of no importance. Rank does not properly apply to the different studies necessary for liberal culture, any more than it applies to the different parts of a watch. There is an important question of relative position, but that is not a question of rank.

Some one may ask here; Has a perfect system of education been framed? Probably not. The human mind is too complicated and delicate a piece of mechanism to be perfectly comprehended. Yet upon this very point have the thoughts of the most intellectual men of the world been concentrated for more than two thousand years. A result has been obtained. That result is embodied substantially in the complete curriculum of study of Lombard University, differing in no material respect from the curriculum of study in the other colleges and universities of the world. Students sometimes think that this course of study is the result of accident or fancy, and that they should be permitted to interrupt it and tear it to pieces whenever and wherever they please, but no greater mistake was ever committed. Let the sciences therefore receive their due share of attention, but let no one suppose that the study of science makes a full grown scholar or properly educated man.

The second thing that has caused classical studies to be underrated, is the richness of modern literature. Why, it is asked, should we go back to follow with Homer the varying fortunes of Troy or the wanderings of Ulysses, while we have upon our shelves such a poem as the Paradise Lost? Why should we hang over the romantic and not altogether credible narrative of Livy, while we have such histories as those of Merivale and Motley and Draper and Froude, and the profound philosophy and sweeping generalizations of the erudite Buckle? I am not unconscious of the force of these questions. I see men before me who would find it difficult to construe a page of Tacitus, but who know a thousand times more about Germany than the very author of the Germania himself. I see before me men who, I suppose, cannot read a word of Plato or Aristotle, but to whom the valuable thoughts of

Plato and Aristotle, and what is more, the valuable thoughts of Descartes and Leibnitz and Spinoza and Schelling, and Hegel, and Cousin, and Locke, and Hamilton are as familiar as the street that leads to market or the names of their children. But these are rare men. They transcend all ordinary rules. Colleges and Universities were not founded for such men, but for the average intellect of such young men as are gathered from year to year within their walls. The superior richness of modern literature, as compared with the ancient, is fully conceded. But the most valuable treasures of modern literature are slightly recondite. Those shelves in our popular libraries upon which the most valuable works stand are generally the least frequented. To appreciate and enjoy them requires not only some little reach of thought but refinement of feeling, and enthusiasm in the pursuit of truth. Now how is a young man or woman of average intellect and ordinary culture to be educated into a taste, not to say passion or enthusiasm, for such authors as Coleridge and DeQuincy and Mill and Spencer and Draper and Emerson? In no way, we think, more effectually than by a course of early classical study. These very men to whom modern literature is so much indebted, have generally been classical scholars. Their taste and style have been formed upon classic models. Those readers whose tastes have been similarly cultivated, and who have drank at the same fountains of inspiration, will necessarily read with a more genial sympathy and appreciation.

The argument urged for the exclusion of classical studies from our schools is that we should thereby get more time for what is called a practical education. Now it is a little remarkable that the advocates of classical studies have never sought to exclude any study which has generally been deemed important as a part of a college course. They alone are in favor of a "liberal education" in the proper sense of those words. But suppose the test of practicalness to be applied as that word is generally understood,—not as disciplinary but as furnishing that information and skill that are useful in the conduct of the practical affairs of life.

Connected with Chicago University is the most powerful telescope of its kind in the world. The devotion to science manifested by those noble men who secured that instrument, has done more to render Chicago illustrious than any other thing that could be mentioned. In that observatory, toward which the eyes of scientific men on both sides of the Atlantic are now turned, presides one of the geniuses of the age. And what is he doing? He is cultivating Practical Astronomy. Now go and examine a page of Prof. Safford's calculations and explain to me, if you can, the connection between that practical work of his and the affairs of Lake street. Tell me, if you can, how far it concerns the gigantic interests of the great city that lies beneath the eye of that observatory whether the parallax of Sirius is one second or somewhat less. To the business interests of that city the displacement of a railroad switch is of far more importance than the parallax of the stars. I do not mean of course that commerce is not indebted to Astronomy. Destroy the sextant and take away our ability to determine a ship's position at sea by an observation on the sun or stars, and nine-tenths of our shipping would be rotting at our wharfs. Astronomy! it has its seat in the heavens, but it touches this daily mortal life of ours in a thousand ways. What I mean to say is, that these higher matters of so-called practical astronomy with which Prof. Safford and the Chicago telescope are concerned to-day, have nothing whatever to do with the practical conduct of the ordinary affairs of life.

The same might be said of the higher Mathematics. They are involved in some practical matters to be sure, but they are not studied by most students for their practical utility. In after life they more readily slip from the memory and are less seldom recurred to than the classics. How many graduates, ten years out of college and actively engaged in business, can demonstrate the problem of the parabola or of the ellipse? Yet these are beautiful problems,—only moderately difficult, and as well calculated as any part of Analytical Geometry to make an impression upon the memory. Not one student in a hundred leaves college for either of the professions or for commerce or the trades who has a thought of ever recurring to his Analytical Geometry or Calculus, unless it may be after many years, as a matter of curiosity, to see how little he knows of that over which he once bent and plodded so many toilsome hours, or to revive the recollections of his struggles for college honors. I would not be understood as maintaining that because this is so these studies are not important. It is no small thing that the mind has once in a life time comprehended the Calculus with its subtle discussions and shadowy principles. The very intangibility and slipperiness of the matters with which it deals, unlike anything with which the mind copes before or afterwards, constitute the chief merit of the study as a gymnastic mental exercise. But the supposed importance of the higher Mathematics on account of their supposed practical utility, has very little foundation in fact. This idea is entertained mostly by persons who do not know what the higher Mathematics are. With Prof. Safford, Algebra, Trigonometry and the Calculus are practical matters. They are involved in his business of enlarging the boundaries of Astronomical Science. For the ordinary professional and business man they are a discipline and nothing more. But that after all is the highest end of education.

I now proceed to show, as best I can, that the classics are both practical and disciplinary. First practical. There is not, it is true, much classical literature that is important to the general reader by reason of the simple facts which it recites; but there is one book that might be denominated a classic which is of transcendent importance, and that is the Greek Testament. There is no reason why every scholar should not be a theologian. Indeed theology so pervades all science and all the highest productions of literature, no true scholar can fail to regard theology as the science of sciences, the grand focus where all other truth should shed some light. Now while we admit that we have great theologians who cannot read the New Testament in the Greek language, such ability is nevertheless a valuable attainment, and especially of late, since attention has been turned so much to the early history of Christianity. Again, the Greek language is the language of science. Three-fourths of our scientific terms, I suppose, are derived from the Greek. The Latin language is the language of the civil law, and no reader of law books is quite at home who does not read Latin. Both Greek and Latin enter largely into the composition of the English language as they do into nearly all the modern languages of Europe.

The basis of the English, to be sure, is the Saxon, but it has been enriched by the Greek and Latin, and no one is prepared to study the English advantageously who has not laid the foundation for such study by a critical knowledge of the classics. The Greek and Latin languages are models of their kind. The ancients studied little else but language. Hence the wonderful perfection of their respective languages. Their adaptation to the expression of nice shades of thought is marvelous. So the power and beauty of the English language has been greatly increased by the introduction of words from the Greek and Latin. Many of these words of classical derivation have a latent signification and beauty which none but a classical scholar readily detects.

Again, the classical scholar becomes critical by comparing his own language with the classic models. It is difficult to become a good judge ot any thing without comparing it with other things of the same kind. By comparing we acquire a taste for critical observing, and this is one of the principal requisitions in the study of language.

Few men ever studied the English language more thoroughly from the stand point of a purely English student than Henry Clay. For seventy years, undistracted by that wider range of study that makes a scholar, he studied American politics and the power of expression in his native tongue. He became, it is conceded, the greatest American orator; but strange to say, as if to mock all attempts at literary, scholarly or rhetorical excellence not founded upon early classical attainments, there is little left to-day of Henry Clay as an orator, except the tradition of his silvery voice, of his majestic presence and of the power of his personal magnetism. The speeches of Webster and Everett, carefully preserved, are conned by every school boy, and will be handed down to the generations that shall come after us a thousand years hence as a portion—as a sacred portion of American classics. If there be anything practical it is the power of expression, —not simply the power to move the hearts of men by oral speech, wherein much is attributable to the magic influence of the human voice; but that greater power which embodies in the written word the best thought of the age, and so clothes that word with universal beauty that it becomes classic, and passes on through the ages, surviving the wreck of empires, and what is more, the rise and fall of whole systems of philosophy, binding together by the living beauty of thought and form the successive generations of men. Practical! What is the world's great treasure but the world's great thought? And what would be the value of that thought but for the vehicle in which it is carried forward and made immortal while the thinkers die?

It was a great thing to build the Chicago tunnel. By it many millions of men and women will yet be blessed. All honor to the science that achieved that result. But it was a greater thing to write Ecce Homo;—to so marry beauty of thought and form as to make a classic upon that most important of all subjects whereby it is hoped that many a thirsty spirit may yet be drawn to the fountains of eternal life.

But the study of the classics is practical not only because it facilitates the study of the English, but because it facilitates the study of the modern languages of Europe generally. There is a disposition at present in many institutions of learning to substitute the modern languages for the ancient. But it would be better to add the modern languages and lengthen the course. The study of the classics is such an excellent preparation for the study of the modern languages, it seems proper to begin with the classics but a pity to stop there. The classical scholar holds the key to untold treasures. Why should he, for the sake of gaining a year or two for commerce or the professions omit to walk in and take possession?

But some one may ask, is there not danger that this refining and re-refining of the taste and feelings,—this profound culture and scholarly enthusiasm, which a prolonged period of study, if well directed, is calculated to secure, will give a disrelish for the dry details and drudgery of business? Is the highest cultivation of the æsthetic and the ideal consistent with the devotion to the practical and real, necessary to secure success in life? This certainly is a grave question, and it cannot be disposed of with a single flourish of the pen. To thoughtful minds it recurs again and again, bringing with it a series of questions, exposing the shallowness of our philosophy, and reaching down into the unfathomable depths of that greatest of all mysteries, the human spirit. How to reconcile the real and the ideal,—how to reconcile the finite and the infinite,—how to bask in God's sunlight of eternal truth and beauty, and sport in the actual liberty of heaven, while the limitations of earth yet hang upon the fettered spirit;—that is the difficulty. But not to put too fine a point on this matter and miss any practical reflection that might be made, we may observe that this antagonism may after all be more apparent than real. The limitations of our earthly lot should be accepted,—freely and joyously accepted. They are doubtless a part of the disciplinary process through which the finite travels towards that state of exaltation and freedom which cannot be fully realized this side of the bounds of time and space.

It is possible to lead two distinct lives side by side, the practical earthly life, and the life of sentiment and emotion. We do in fact, all of us lead such lives, however dwarfed and feeble one or both of them may be, and these lives supplement each other. And if they be so accepted and cultivated, and developed into rounded fullness and beauty, the antagonism will largely disappear and they will so blend and harmonize as to afford a dim prophecy of that life wherein all things will be blended in one grand and harmonious unity. The men who have most challenged our admiration have been men who have combined ability for practical affairs with scholarly culture and attainments. Cicero was a statesman, and a man of letters and an orator. Julius Cæsar was the greatest soldier of his age. But while he was pushing the conquering eagles of Rome to the pillars of Hercules on the west, and the highlands of Caledonia on the north, he was writing those immortal Commentaries wherein fifteen centuries after the Roman power is swept from the countries which he conquered, the scholar traces with ever new and undiminished delight the history of Cæsar's brilliant campaigns. Edmund Burke was an illustrious example of a man, the luster of whose fame shines with a double light. Parliamentary speeches are usually the dullest of reading after the occasion is passed which inspired them, and the circumstances are partially forgotten. But that orator is never dull who speaks in the double capacity of statesman and philosopher. Our own late lamented Everett was honored with nearly all the most important of offices within the gift of the people or the appointment of the government. He was successively Representative in Congress, Governor of Massachusetts, Minister to the Court of St. James, Secretary of State and U. S. Senator. At the same time he was recognized as one of the ripest and most accomplished of American scholars. These men, quite as much as any men that have lived, bore upon their shoulders the weight of the world's great business, but they turned aside ever and anon to refresh their wearied spirits in the pursuits of philosophy and letters, carrying back with them the ideal into the real, and thus elevating, beautifying and idealizing everything that touches human interests. Compared with such men the scholarly monk of the middle ages becomes almost contemptible. He would indeed be quite so, but for the service which he rendered in preserving the very literature whose claims we are advocating,

—a literature which, when dragged from the monkish cell and studied by the men of the world, gave the world that impulse which has resulted in our modern civilization with all its wealth of science, literature and art. Nothing could be more unfortunate than that scholarly culture and attainments should again be divorced from the discipline and experience of practical life. If the day shall come when the interests of letters shall be re-committed to men devoted exclusively to scholarly pursuits, from that day we shall begin to travel back towards the civilization of mediæval Europe. There is not only no proper antagonism between culture and the executive ability which administers the practical affairs of the world, but they aid each other as has been demonstrated by every year of the world's history since Constantinople was taken by the Turks, and the scholars of the east were dispersed with their manuscripts through western Europe, introducing the polished learning of the east to the modern practical European mind.

That young men should usually graduate from college with a lack of worldly prudence and a distaste for business should be expected. And that the world should move right on just as if the young men aforesaid had not graduated at all, should also be expected. It is a stern old world, with a touch of conservatism, and does not ordinarily yield its highest prizes to school boys. It will not even stop, my young friend, to look at your diploma. It does not care for it. You might about as well leave it behind you. It will soon become lumber. But no true young man will be permanently disheartened. Those of you who have completed the entire course of study pursued in this institution instead of taking a partial course as you might have done, have evinced a certain constitutional thoroughness which gives hope of success. It may also be said that the force of will called into exercise in keeping yourselves up to the standard of scholarship necessary to enable you to pass the requisite examinations has generated force of character, which again is reinforced by a habit of steady persistent effort, constituting altogether the surest possible guaranty of success. You have attempted one important thing in life and have accomplished it. You go into the world with that courage and stability which a well earned and complete victory gives an inexperienced soldier. No one who has taken a partial course can have quite the same feeling. You who have been through the complete course have laid the foundation of your education deep and strong. You have come to dislike cheap and unsubstantial things. They do not consist with those mental habits and tastes which you have formed during the years of study and thorough discipline which you have passed through. Among all your learning you have learned one thing perhaps more important than all else—no student goes through an entire college course without learning it—and that is, that while you may be credited occasionally for what is a matter of luck, it is unreliable through a period of time, and that there is no permanent success that is not earned. You have also discovered that the correlate of the proposition is equally true:—that no well directed, persistent effort will finally fail of its reward. These ideas, the most valuable with which a young man can enter life, a thorough course of classical study cannot fail to inculcate. A thoroughly educated young man does not aim at a meteoric reputation. But he is found among those who are gradually and noiselessly feeling their way to permanent professional or commercial success. He has acquired a taste for the gradual, the noiseless and the permanent.

These are some of the more obvious advantages which a liberally educated man enjoys. They are the advantages that have a practical bearing, and upon which he may predicate his hopes of material success. But there are other advantages that are to be measured by a different standard.

A pitiful object is a human being who can see no value in anything that cannot be measured by dollars and cents. Yet the world is full of such men. They regard a life as a comparative failure that has not been blessed with worldly thrift. They have no maxims of conduct for young men, except such as relate to economy, industry and business success. Worldly prudence constitutes the religion of these men. It presides over all the affairs of their households. It constitutes the atmosphere in which their children are raised. In its name the school houses are built and in its name, I had almost said, the very altar of God is erected. Now what makes these men unlovely? They are not destitute of positive merits. They constitute the back bone of American society. They own the rail roads and the banks and the elevators, and they built the identical churches to which you and I proudly point as the result and sign of our christian civilization. But they lack sentiment and emotion. They lack the ideal which raises man from the thraldom of the actual, and exalts him to the realm of the possible. It would benefit them some to read a good novel if they could be affected by it, for their emotional nature is a waste. They go to church to be sure, and but for the fact that they go there for the express purpose of setting a good example before their clerks and children, and of getting religion as a matter of prudence, they might sometimes be moved by the presentation of spiritual truth, and be induced, for the moment at least, to accept religion for religion's sake,—for its own blessed immediate reality. But they have cultivated only the outlooking, the observing faculties. The reflective and introspective faculties are dormant; the emotions are awakened only by the sensuous; and the spiritual nature is a waste. It is with difficulty that they can see any other than the outward, material world. They are inclined to think that the literal body will be raised, that heaven is a place, and that the joys of heaven are not inappropriately set forth under the imagery of golden crowns and golden streets. This is the penalty doubtless which God inflicts on men who through the period of a lifetime cultivate only the outlooking faculties and violate the eternal laws of the spirit. To observe, to strengthen the power of observing and to know the material world in all its relations and aptitudes is the present tendency of the American mind. And what is the drift of American scholarship? That too is in the same direction. It is scienceward. And even the more abstract and disciplinary sciences, the Mathematics, Astronomy and Mechanical Philosophy, are beginning to give way to those that afford more scope for the observing faculties, and bring the scholar into more intimate acquaintance with the material world. The great thing now is to search out and be able to know all the flowers and plants and reptiles and birds and insects on the face of the earth, and to call them by their names. That is modern scholarship.

Far be it from me to disparage the study of Natural History. It has its place in every complete education. But Natural History is a child's study. In children the observing powers are active and the reflective are not. Nature dictates that the observing powers of children should have full scope. It would be difficult perhaps to over educate a child in that direction. The knowledge gathered is not only what the young mind craves, but the process of the education if properly conducted takes the child abroad into the open air and sunshine, where in sympathy with Nature and all her genial influences he may grow up naturally as a child should grow.

Who of us have not been touched with that beautiful little poem of Longfellow's in which Agassiz is represented as the child of Nature.

And Nature the dear old nurse, took
  The child upon her knee
Saying, "Here is a story book
  Thy father has written for thee.

Come, wander with me," she said,
  "Into regions yet untrod,
And read what is still unread
  In the manuscripts of God."

And he wandered away and away,
  With Nature, the dear old nurse,
Who sang to him night and day
  The rhymes of the universe.

But the time comes when we should listen to other rhymes and read other manuscripts than those of the physical creation. The introspective faculties must be developed, and that is done by the study of mental and moral philosophy, logic, art, criticism and philology. If we stop short of these studies mental balance is lost; the noblest part of our nature lies dormant, and we fall inevitably into the deplorable drift and tendency of the American mind. What we want is a corrective of our over cultivated observing powers, and over practical, materialistic tendency. If there be any element of scholarship that can serve as such corrective, that is the element upon which emphasis is to be placed. We believe such element is to be found in the study of the ancient classics.

That study brings the mind directly back upon itself. The material world is lost sight of. We deal with thought. Whatever beauties charm us are the beauties of thought. That thought is given us in a foreign word. Often there is no

English word that expresses it. In such case we swing aloof from the foreign word and holding the thought directly before the mind unsupported by any word we go in search of an English expression, and while searching we weigh, balance and discriminate. We call into exercise the reason, the imagination, the judgment, the taste and the memory; the exercise constituting altogether the finest mental discipline that could be devised. The study of Mathematics to be sure calls into exercise the reasoning powers. So chaste and severe are the demonstrations, it is invaluable as a discipline. It can do for the mind what the study of the classics cannot, but it is equally true that the study of the classics can do what the study of Mathematics cannot. Both discipline the reasoning powers, but how different the kinds of reasoning. The one concerns only numbers and quantity. The other embraces the whole field of human thought, motives and passions. The classical student has no unbending formula upon which he can rely to conduct him to absolute truth. The quantities with which he deals are too variable even for the application of the Calculus. He cannot translate a page without the exercise of his reasoning powers, but the factors which enter into his calculations are grammatical dependence, logical sequence, historic truth, poetic beauty, and all the accumulated treasures of Geography, Ethnography and Archæology. What possible exercise of the reasoning powers can be comparable to that, whereby the student in a foreign and strangely constructed language gropes his way amid the glorious monuments of the world's past achievements in thought and deed? The disciplinary effect of classical studies is strictly and properly culture. Where the reason shades off into taste, where the reason shades off into judgment, where the reason underlies the imagination, affording it its surest support and control, there the disciplinary effect of classical studies is realized, and that constitutes culture.

Then there is the classic spirit of the ancient Greeks and Romans that has charmed the world for so many ages. Says Dr. Temple in his clebrated essay of the "Essays and Reviews," speaking of the ancient Greeks and Romans; "It is not their genius only which makes them attractive, it is the classic life of the people of that day. It is the image there only to be seen of our highest matured powers in their freshest vigor; it is the unattainable grace of the prime of manhood; it is the pervading sense of youthful beauty. The common workmen of those times breathed the air of the Gods. To combine the highest powers of the intellect with the freshness of youth, was possible only once, and that is the glory of the classic nations. The inspiration which is drawn by man from the memory of those whom he loved and admired in the spring time of life is drawn by the world now from the study of Greece and Rome."

The same spirit which pervaded their literature pervaded their art. Bayard Taylor, speaking of the yet unshaken columns of the Parthenon, says: "In their perfect symmetry was solved the enigma of that harmony which is the very being of God and the operation of his laws. Those blocks of sunny marble were piled upon each other to the chorus of the same song which the seasons sing in their ordered round, and the planets in their balanced orbits. But the rythmic pulsations of that jubilant religion have died away and earth will never see another Parthenon." For the same reason we may say; earth will never see another Iliad. To us the spirit of that art and that literature is especially important. De Tocqueville says: "No literature places those fine qualities in which the writers of democracies are naturally deficient, in bolder relief than that of the ancients; no literature therefore," he says, "ought to be more studied in democratic times."

That is, the idea, I may observe, in conclusion, which fifty years ago took so strong a hold of the mind of the great apostle of American democracy, the sage of Monticello. Having devoted his life to combatting the political ideas of the old world; warring upon caste and privilege; breaking down the administration of Adams because it exhibited, as he thought, too much of the spirit which animated the governing classes of England; recognizing in every fellow citizen an American sovereign; not satisfied with having endowed him with the ballot to be counted, but anxious to so elevate him as to give him a potential voice in the affairs of the nation; we find him in those last halcyon days of his retirement—his political battles all fought and won, enshrined in a nation's heart, the din of party strife reverberating in the distance—we find him no longer thinking of politics, but of the classical education needed by his democratic countrymen, and engaged in accomplishing what he deemed the crowning achievement of his life, the founding of the University of Virginia. There are men still living who saw the aged patriarch as he was accustomed to sit in the portico of his elevated country seat, overlooking the institution which his brain had conceived and his munificence had aided to endow, his heart still warm, and beating as ever responsive to the great heart of the American people, with a clearness of mental vision that made him almost prophetic as he cast the horoscope of the future of America, and foresaw that the highest style of American democracy would necessarily include the wisdom and culture of the schools. Such was the vision of the venerable seer after all other objects of earthly interest had faded from his view.

While, therefore, the American people shall cherish the

political principles of Jefferson, let them not forget the connection which he thought he saw between the full fruition of democratic ideas, and the liberality and polish and culture which result from an acquaintance with the art and literature of the polished nations of antiquity.

www.ingramcontent.com/pod-product-compliance
Lightning Source LLC
LaVergne TN
LVHW011138110826
845150LV00008B/2391

* 9 7 8 1 4 1 8 1 9 3 8 3 6 *